Fireflies

by Caroline Arnold
illustrated by Pamela Johnson

SCHOLASTIC INC.
New York   Toronto   London   Auckland   Sydney

The summer air is warm and moist as night falls. Soon bright spots of light begin to shine out of the darkness. First one, then another, flashes among the grass and trees. Each light is a firefly. Blink, blink it flashes. Blink, blink replies another firefly. These amazing insects are like tiny living flashlights. They are sending messages to each other.

Fireflies live in many parts of the world. In the United States and Canada, you can find fireflies east of the Rocky Mountains. You are most likely to see them on warm nights when the moon is not shining.

ROCKY MOUNTAINS

UNITED STATES

If you hold out your hand, a firefly might land on it. The firefly will be about as big as the end of your little finger.

There are more than 2,000 species of fireflies in the world.

male firefly

female firefly

6

Fireflies belong to the group of insects called beetles. (Ladybugs and water beetles are two other kinds of beetles.) All beetles have two pairs of wings. One pair is used for flying. The other pair of wings is hard. They help the beetle balance when it is flying. When the beetle rests, the hard wings fold over the top of its body and protect it.

Male fireflies are strong fliers. But females do not fly very much. The females of a few kinds have no wings and do not fly at all. Female fireflies are bigger than males.

Some people call fireflies lightning bugs because their flashes look like little bursts of lightning. Each flash of the firefly's light lasts about half a second. The firefly may flash just once, or in a series of flashes. The color, timing, and length of the flashes are a coded message. The flashes say what kind of firefly it is, and whether it is a male or female.

One of the most common fireflies in the United States is called *Photinus pyralis* (fo-TY-nus pi-RAL-is). It usually flashes once every six or seven seconds. When the male turns on his light, he swoops in the air. The streak of light looks like the letter J.

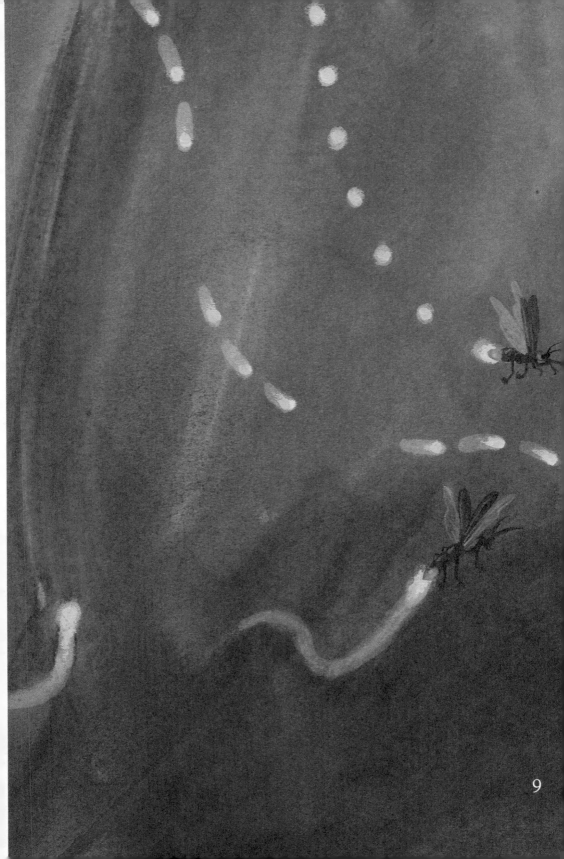

The part of the firefly that makes light is called its lantern. It is at the back of the firefly's body. The lantern is so bright that several fireflies together can make enough light to read a book or take a photo.

A firefly has two special chemicals in its body. They are luciferin (loo-SIF-eh-ruhn) and luciferase (loo-SIF-eh-ras). The firefly also has a chemical called ATP. All living things have ATP. ATP in your body provides energy to move your muscles. When the firefly's ATP mixes with luciferin, luciferase, and oxygen from the air, the chemical reaction makes light.

The light made by a firefly has almost no heat. You can touch a firefly and it will be cool.

Fireflies are active mostly at night. Flashing lights help fireflies find each other in the dark. A firefly can mate only with another firefly of its own kind, or species. The coded flashes help fireflies of the same species to recognize one another.

A female firefly usually stays near the ground. She perches on a leaf or a blade of grass.

The male begins his search for a female at dusk. He flashes his light as he flies. The light sends a signal to other fireflies. It says, "Here I am. I am a male and I am looking for a mate."

The large eyes of a firefly help it to see well.

When a female sees the male's light, she flashes her own signal. She says, "I'm down here. Come and find me." The male flies closer and flashes his light again. She answers again. They repeat their messages over and over. Soon they find each other, and then mate.

13

After a female firefly mates with a male, she is ready to lay her eggs. She waits for the dark of night. Then she crawls under a leaf. The eggs come out of a small tube at the back of the female's body. This tube is called an ovipositor (oh-vee-POS-ih-tur). The eggs stick to the leaf. (Some fireflies lay their eggs on moss or on grass instead.)

A female firefly lays about 100 tiny eggs. Each one is about the size of a period on this page. The female may lay eggs for several nights in a row. Then she is finished.

Inside each egg, a new firefly is growing. It will hatch in about four weeks.

A firefly has four stages in its life. The first stage is an egg. When the egg hatches, the insect enters its second stage. It has become a larva (LAR-vuh). Larvae (LAR-vee) is the word for more than one larva. A larva has no wings. Its body is long. (A caterpillar is the larva stage of a butterfly.)

A firefly larva looks like a tiny, wiggly worm. It is less than one eighth of an inch long. But it already has tiny lights. It has one light on each side of its body. People sometimes call firefly larvae glowworms.

The firefly larva crawls along the ground and looks for food. It finds small insects, snails, and worms. The larva kills them with its poisonous bite. Then it eats them.

Only a few larvae grow to be adult fireflies. Many larvae are eaten by birds and other animals. They are not hurt by the firefly larva's poison.

The larva grows so much in its first month that its skin no longer fits. The skin splits, and the larva wiggles out of it. A new, bigger skin is underneath. This process is called molting. A larva molts about six times in its life.

When fall comes, the firefly larva crawls under a rock and rests for the winter. Then when the weather warms up in spring, it comes out. It eats and grows all summer. Then it rests for the winter again. The next spring, the firefly larva wakes up and eats for just a few weeks. Then it is ready for the next stage of its life.

The firefly larva digs a shallow hole in the ground. It crawls into the hole and covers itself. A liquid from the larva's skin soaks into the dirt. It makes a hard shell around the larva. Then the larva curls up and rests.

The body of the larva is changing inside its skin. About five weeks later, the skin molts for the last time. Now the larva has become a pupa (PEW-puh). It is in its third stage of life.

The pupa has begun to grow wings. The pupa stays inside the dirt hole. Each day it grows and changes. About ten days later it has become an adult firefly. It has reached the fourth and last stage of its life.

The process insects go through as they grow from an egg to an adult is called metamorphosis (met-uh-MOR-fuh-sis). Metamorphosis is a Greek word that means change.

The adult firefly rests in its hole for a few more days. Then it is ready to break out and fly.

The adult firefly comes out of its hole nearly two years after it began life as an egg. It chews the dirt to make an opening. Then it pushes itself out with its legs. The firefly waits for night. Then it will stretch its wings and begin its search for a mate.

Adult fireflies live for only a few weeks. They die after mating and laying eggs.

Fireflies drink water. But most adult fireflies do not eat. They live on food that was stored in their bodies when they were larvae.

A few kinds of adult fireflies do eat. Some of these belong to a group called *Photuris* (fo-TUR-us). (Several species of *Photuris* live in the United States.) The female *Photuris* gets food by tricking other species of fireflies. If a male of another species flashes, she copies his signal. She pretends to be a female of his species. When he flies down, she eats him.

Most male fireflies search for mates alone. But the males of some kinds of fireflies work together to attract females. Hundreds of males gather in trees or large bushes. They adjust the timing of their flashes so that all of their lights go on and off at the same time. Then the whole tree blinks on and off like a giant neon sign. When females see the huge light, they come and find a mate.

People in Central and South America sometimes catch fireflies and put them in net bags. They use the fireflies as lamps. Sometimes they wear them as glowing decorations.

Firefly festivals are celebrated in Japan every summer. People catch fireflies and put them in cages. Then they take the fireflies in boats to the middle of a lake or river. All at once the people open the cages. The air sparkles with thousands of firefly lights.

Fireflies are not the only living things that can make their own light. Some kinds of fish, clams, worms, bacteria, and even mushrooms are able to glow. All of them use chemicals in their bodies to make light. Their lights may be yellow, green, blue, red, or orange. Living things that make their own light are called bioluminescent (bi-oh-loo-meh-NES-ehnt). Scientists study fireflies and other bioluminescent creatures to learn more about them.

You can enjoy watching fireflies flicker on the grass or in the woods on a warm summer evening. The glow of the fireflies' lights seems like magic. It is amazing to know that they use their light to "talk" to one another.

Index

About the Author

Caroline Arnold is the author of more than eighty books for children, including award-winning titles such as *Koala*, *Saving the Peregrine Falcon*, and *Dinosaur Mountain*. When she was growing up in Minneapolis, Minnesota, she spent her summers at a camp in northern Wisconsin. That is where she first developed her interest in animals and the out-of-doors.

Today she goes to zoos, museums, and wildlife parks as part of the research for her books. Ms. Arnold lives in Los Angeles, California, with her husband, who is a neuroscientist, and their two children. Ms. Arnold also teaches part-time in the Writers' Program at UCLA Extension.

If You Want to Read More About Fireflies:

Animals That Glow, by Judith Janda Presnall (Franklin Watts, 1993).

Fireflies, by Sylvia A. Johnson (Lerner Publications, 1986).

Fireflies, by Joanne Ryder (Harper Collins, 1977).

Nature's Living Lights: Fireflies and Other Bioluminescent Creatures, by Alvin and Virginia Silverstein (Little Brown and Company, 1988).

Library of Congress Cataloging-in-Publication Data

Arnold, Caroline.
Fireflies / by Caroline Arnold; illustrated by Pamela Johnson.
p.   cm.
Includes bibliographical references and index.
ISBN 0-590-46944-4
1. Fireflies — Juvenile literature. [1. Fireflies.]
I. Johnson, Pamela, ill. II. Title.
QL596.L28A76 1994
597.76′44 — dc20
93-30439
CIP
AC

12 11 10 9 8 7 6 5 4 3 2 1   4 5 6 7 8/9

Printed in the U.S.A.   23

First Scholastic printing, May 1994

Book design by Laurie McBarnette